T0105702

Whispering Wings

MY WALK WITH GOD

ANGELCIA CAROL WRIGHT

BALBOA.
PRESS
A DIVISION OF HAY HOUSE

Copyright © 2012 Angelcia Carol Wright

All rights reserved. No part of this book may be used or reproduced by any means, graphic, electronic, or mechanical, including photocopying, recording, taping or by any information storage retrieval system without the written permission of the publisher except in the case of brief quotations embodied in critical articles and reviews.

ISBN: 978-1-4525-5944-5 (sc)
ISBN: 978-1-4525-5945-2 (hc)
ISBN: 978-1-4525-5943-8 (e)

Library of Congress Control Number: 2012918210

Balboa Press books may be ordered through booksellers or by contacting:

Balboa Press
A Division of Hay House
1663 Liberty Drive
Bloomington, IN 47403
www.balboapress.com
1-(877) 407-4847

Because of the dynamic nature of the Internet, any web addresses or links contained in this book may have changed since publication and may no longer be valid. The views expressed in this work are solely those of the author and do not necessarily reflect the views of the publisher, and the publisher hereby disclaims any responsibility for them.

The author of this book does not dispense medical advice or prescribe the use of any technique as a form of treatment for physical, emotional, or medical problems without the advice of a physician, either directly or indirectly. The intent of the author is only to offer information of a general nature to help you in your quest for emotional and spiritual well-being. In the event you use any of the information in this book for yourself, which is your constitutional right, the author and the publisher assume no responsibility for your actions.

Any people depicted in stock imagery provided by Thinkstock are models, and such images are being used for illustrative purposes only.
Certain stock imagery © Thinkstock.

Printed in the United States of America

Balboa Press rev. date: 10/09/2012

Table of Contents

I Walked With The Angels

Dreams and faraway lands surround me.

As I drift into another world.

A Band of Angels greet me with their

Beautiful Wings unfurled.

Each one came forward with an outreached hand

I eagerly put my hand in theirs

And I waited what they planned.

The Angel's wings radiated

And their colors seeped into my soul.

Love filled my heart and absorbed me

It was the color of Gold.

The Angel of sorrow is green.

The Angel deals with the Envious and Mean.

The Angel in blue came on the scene

Together they made a good team.

Along the way was marred

With lost souls who had never cried for their God

I observed their plight and I cried at the sight
As we walked through the Garden of Life.
The next Angel waved a spray,
Smelled like lavender, it's hard to say,
Then truth answered my questions as
Peace was my lesson.

Then the Angel of Death was in sight holding onto my gaze
with such might. Fear swirled its clutches around my soul
as it started to close in upon its goal. My eyes were fixated
at this sight when another Angel appeared before me so
bright. She reached out for my hand and pulled me up and
surrounded my spirit in light.

Because I walked with the Best, I passed the test. When I
walked with the Angels Last Night!

Special Thanks

To The Four Sisters

Several years ago, my three sisters and I decided to write about whatever interested each one of us personally. Our maiden name is Hall. There were eight of us. There were four brothers, all who have died before us, except Raymond who is our youngest brother. Two of my sisters are divorced and two of us are married. We are called the Four Sisters.

Each one of us has our own unique and different style in our writings. We all have a lot we want to share with our children, grandchildren, our family and our friends.

Barbara Adkins has written many "How to Books" and she is great at researching and publishing Ancestry books. She is also a recognized artist. There is a Cherokee line in our ancestry and Barbara is known as 'Little doe" among Indian circles.

Barbara has even found a line of royalty in our line. We haven't let that sink in yet.

Barbara has a unique talent in which she makes these beautiful pine needle baskets and she is one of very few people left who teaches this lost art.

Sandra Moore has found herself in her love for animals and her crafts. Her books, consisting of a special doggie cook book and her children's book on parrots is very popular. A project she is experimenting with now includes many recipes she has tried out and remembers from childhood. She also is an artist.

Joyce Timberlake is a Virginia artist who is well known as an art teacher and story teller. Her lifelong project, "Whoever Heard of a Purple Happy Tree", a children's book is about to go to press. This is a story about a little Eco tree who tries to save the environment and the world. The Happy Tree is his name. There will be many drawings and paintings included in this book. This is only one of many children stories by this popular artist and it should be published this year. When I was searching for the perfect name for my book, I consulted with my sisters on several occasions. Barbara suggested the name should have "Wings" in the title. Sandra, who we call Sandy, liked "Spirit Wings" and when I mentioned it to Joyce she told me that one time she had a chapter with Ducks Unlimited called "The Whispering Wings". She was not involved with it any longer and she asked me if I wanted to use it. I said, "Yes! It is perfect." Together we decided "Whispering Wings" represented what I had been shown and this name could describe the book better than any other name.

As for me, I go by Carol Wright, and for years my family and I have been involved in a business which takes most of my time. I always thought as I get older I would have more time for myself, but it doesn't work that way, the older I get the busier I get. All I know is before I experienced this walk with GOD I had searched for years for my purpose in life and GOD finally answered my questions and more. This is my Walk with God.

I don't know how I ever found time to write. When I first had an OBE (out of body experience), it was after we lost everything in a house fire. None of us were hurt, thank GOD. We didn't have insurance and it took us over 2 years to rebuild our home.

During that time someone started stalking me. I never could prove who I thought it was. The person would tap on my window at night only when my husband wasn't at home. It wasn't that long ago but it was before everyone had cell phones. We didn't have a phone so I could not call for help. The next morning there would be a heart drawn on one of the windows outside. If that was all that was done I might have been able to stand the pressure but the heart drawn on the window would be drawn in blood. Then my animals would mysteriously die. My boys had two rabbits. They were kept outside in a cage in the back yard. We had them for years. One morning I walked out to the cage and both of them were on the ground next to the cage. Their stomachs were slit open. A week later I couldn't find my cat so I started looking for it everywhere. I found it in the kids small swimming pool face down. He was dead. Have you ever tried to give a cat a bath? Cats hate water. This was one of those small round pools. The cat would have jumped out of it before he would have drowned. I know someone had to have held him down under the water until he drowned. I know this was not an accidental. Every animal I had found a strange death, just in 2 years.

I finally decided not to ever get another animal until this was over. I felt angry and I always thought I will catch whoever it was who was stalking me, but I never did.

Finally when we moved the stalking stopped and my life returned to normal. It was as though someone wanted to see me upset.

At this same time in my life, I had never heard of having an out of body experience. After it happened to me I asked everyone if they had any idea what it could have been. No one seemed to know. I couldn't find any books on this subject either. I guess I just didn't know where to look.

I searched the bible. I even asked a psychic. No one had an answer that even sounded reasonable.

After GOD lifted the veil and revealed everything to me I have found books on every subject and of every possible experience imaginable and now with the internet you can find anything you want. At that time I was not ready to learn or I just did not understand that is until God started answering my questions. I guess I am getting everything I ask for, whether I like it or not. I now know I evidently planned my life this way before I came here on this adventure.

THE COVER

This cover symbolizes each period of time in my life until I reached my time of complete awareness.

The wings represent my searching for truth all these years. The different color streamers represent the colors of the levels and awareness of my life.

The spiral represents the orb which surrounds each and every spirit and contains all of the lives and experiences of each individual spirit in their each individual orb from the beginning of time.

Joyce Timberake, Artist Designed the cover

FORWARD

A famous singer once wrote a book about a seagull that could never fly high enough to satisfy his own soul. No matter how high he flew it was never high enough. Every time he got a chance he had to prove to himself he could fly higher than any other gull. This gull wanted to know what his purpose in life was and just how high he could go. If the sky was there why couldn't he get to the top? This seagull was not satisfied sitting on a pier somewhere and fishing. He did not want to fly along with the other gulls. The other gulls tried to get him to come along, but this seagull was not satisfied until he could prove what he thought was his purpose in life. In the end this seagull flew so high he was never seen again. Some say he went to the other side.

This seagull represents us in our flight to find GOD. On the other side is HEAVEN which is our main home. On the other side is where we are closer to God and where together choices are made for each of us whether to come to earth or not.

If you decide to come to Earth you will choose a spirit guide who some call your (Guardian Angel) and together with GOD'S help you will chart the course you want to follow through the life you are about to undertake.

We pick our family because they will support us or help us make the right decisions along the way. In some cases we may choose someone who in their own way may cause you extreme pain, but it may be the only way you could have learned the important lesson(s) that you chose to improve upon and/or lessons you needed to learn.

All these lessons we go through will help make us graduate into a more perfect soul and closer to be one with GOD when we return. This should always be our goal.

The mind controls our physical body. The Spirit controls our soul. The spirit dominates every life they soul lives whether or not in the flesh. The spirit waits for the mind to accept its existence. The spirit will throw hints along the way trying to wake up the mind. Even your spirit guide(s) will talk to you from time to time. When the mind finally discovers its own spirit the trumpets in Heaven sound off for all to hear.

ORBS

Life Can Change On a Dime

WHAT DOES "LIFE CAN CHANGE ON A dime even mean"? We automatically understand the underlying message it represents. In theoretical or paranormal circles it means a "turning point". The use of a dime to illustrate standing on its side is a perfect example of our lives. In an instance, circumstances can fall either way, for the good or for the bad. This brings us to the purpose of this saying, with the right knowledge at a predetermined time, even in a blink of an eye or a in a flip of a coin, things can change forever. When life changes on a dime it becomes a life changing phenomenon.

I had never thought of "ORBS" until about three years ago. I was privileged to be in their presence for three or four hours in order to observe them. At the time I didn't know what they were. I had no idea the importance of this discovery. Each one looked like an amazing illuminated spiral floating and moving through the air. Each one was a different size, from 1 inch to 4 inches or more. I took pictures of them to show and prove what I saw.

Afterwards I found out so many other people had seen them. Some people say it was just a moisture drop on my digital camera. The only problem with this was I was watching and following them over a period of hours. Researchers say they are easier to see now with digital photo- graph. It's a lot easier than it was years ago.

I found it is believed these are spirits who want us to know they exist.

I also found out the location where I saw all of these orbs floating are the remains of the old Confederate grounds where soldiers had fought and died in the Civil War.

You have to tell the orbs you want them to show themselves, they want you to see them. In the meantime check your photographs you already have and you may be surprised when you see an orb or two in them.

I found orbs in my old non digital photographs. Research it and find out for yourself.

Once as I sat outside in a chair on a beautiful warm day, I kept hearing a fluttering sound, but couldn't quite place it or see anything. I sat real still and looked around. All of a sudden within 5 inches from my face was a transparent object and it sounded like it had wings which were fluttering. This thing was looking me straight in the eye. It was observing me, I guess. It stayed in one place for about 10 seconds before it disappeared. Suddenly it came back to the same place in front of me and reappeared again.

This was amazing to me. What was so amazing was I could see clear through it. I could see an inner form of some kind. I couldn't quite tell what it was. It was about the size of a dragon fly and it did have wings that were invisible. I know because I could hear them fluttering. I could even feel a slight breeze and I could see the insides which looked like a skeleton. I wouldn't have been able to take a picture of it even if I had my camera with me because it disappeared too fast.

After a lot of research I could not find out anything about the object I had seen but I did publish a book on "ORBS". But, as I said don't take my word for it, check it out. Even at this time I didn't know the importance of orbs.

This idea of orbs has been around for years. Even though I had never heard of ORBS I found a lot of information on them.

In the book I used a lot of "what ifs". I have since found out "what ifs" do not have any importance and should not be used because everything already is, always has been and always will be!

What a deep subject. Where have I heard this before? The Bible. In fact if you read the Bible and try to incorporate what I say in this book you can find the same answers or even the scripture makes more sense.

After many years of the study of different religions I find so many things I was taught or had learned was not completely correct. It never felt right, either. It never hurts to read the bible over and over. You learn something new every time you do. I have read the BIBLE at least three times, as well as read many, many passages over the years just trying to help me to survive. I can always find an answer for my problem in the bible. In Church I was taught there was only God the Father. I was taught if I did anything wrong like dancing I would rot in hell. And I was also taught if I ever sewed anything on Sunday I would have to take each stitch out with my nose in hell when I died. I always hoped this was not true. I was taught to fear GOD. I know in the Catholic religion there is a Mother God. I know there is Jesus the Son. The Holy Bible states we are created in their own image. I never found what that phrase meant. And I never found what I was looking for in the different church's I attended over the years.

I always wondered what my purpose in life was. I had never found the answers I was looking for.

I now know God is a loving God and none of these teachings could possibly have been true.

Discovering Orbs is an important part of LIFE.

Orbs show up in photographs especially ones taken at a gathering of people. They show up in pictures of baby showers or Bridal showers. One picture I took looks like a form of an angel. As I said, I published a book "What are Orbs?" In it I explained how researchers say Orbs have been around for many years. They say you can't see them with the naked eye, but I did. I had never heard of an orb before they started floating out of the woods across from my front yard. I wondered as I watched them from my kitchen window, "what in the world is that?" I was washing dishes and I watched them for about 20 minutes before I couldn't stand it anymore. Finally I stopped cleaning and I got my camera and went outside where I stayed for a couple of hours shooting pictures and watching them come out of the woods and fly up over my house. At first I thought they were some kind of florescent firefly. As I looked around I saw a few in trees and in an azalea bush next to my porch. Some looked like they were posing for me. I found out they are seen mainly around funerals and graveyards, outings and places where there are a lot of people gathered. I can remember thinking at the time I had seen them before when I didn't have a camera with me, but I do now. Later I thought I know I have never seen them before. I did see them somewhere before but didn't remember it until now.

I now know I saw them on the levels but could not take their picture that time. Some say I wrote this in my chart before I came here and it was like De j vu.

After my brother David died I was lying in bed about 6 am one Sunday morning. It was still dark outside when suddenly David was standing in front of me clear as a picture. He had his hands on his hips and he had his right leg up on a piece of firewood. He had on a pair of shorts and a V neck tee shirt. His clothes were gray. The oddest thing he was wearing was bright blue socks. I asked him out loud where did he get those socks?

I said it because I wanted him to know I see him!

He stood looking at me long enough for me to see where he was standing. He was standing in front of our garage where we had just cut down a tree and we were getting ready to split the wood. He had a look on his face of bewilderment, like he wanted to know where he was. He had always come to me for help when he was in trouble. Soon as daylight came I went outside and found the exact location where he had been standing. He knew I would see him and give him some answers. I took a picture of this exact spot.

We talked for about an hour and I told him what was shown to me. I told him this was how he had planned his life and I explained the levels and what was expected of him now and what he must do. I had told him some of the things that had happened to me when he was alive, but David is like a lot of men who won't really listen about anything to do with death. But now he wants to learn.

It must have helped him because he has not come to me since that day. This picture shows a bright orb in the lower center of the picture.

My brother also came to Linda, his wife, a few months after he died. She said he was standing at the end of her bed glaring at her and he held two lightning bolts, one in each hand. One was bright gold and one was a bright blue. She was so upset and she did not understand what he wanted. I told her he probably wanted her to know he was upset for leaving her so soon. David had developed diabetes and was having a lot of trouble and he had gotten where he couldn't work. As soon as his problems began to solve themselves he died. I told Linda he wanted her to know he now has eternal knowledge and now knows what life is all about. This was represented by the gold lightning bolt and the blue lightning bolt proved his body is now healed.

Below is an orange orb I took at the beach.

It looks like the reflection of the sun,
but it was cloudy that day.

Above is the orb that looks like an angel.

Below are orbs at a baby shower.

The top picture is my niece Angelicia, at the beach.

*This picture shows orbs coming out of
the woods across from my home*

Whispering Wings

The Spirit

Patiently awaiting its escape
From a tightly woven web...
A web perfectly spun with God's golden thread.
The thread disappears
As the spirit leaves the ground...
Allowing the Spirit to be Free again...
Heaven Bound

AFTER MANY YEARS OF SEARCHING, GOD CAME to me one night and GOD infused me with an awareness of life I had always searched for. After this happened I developed a hunger for knowledge I had never known. If this has ever happened to you, you will know what I mean. I mean I could not read enough, I could not find out enough information to satisfy my curiosity. If anyone had ever tried to explain this feeling before it had ever happened to me, I would never have known or understood what this feeling was like.

I liken it to being saved.

Many times I asked others in the church "What does it feel like or how do you know if you are Saved"? No answer was good enough for me.

I felt like no one could give me the right answer, until I met this sweet lady. She was 90 years old. She said, "When it happens you will know!" Each one of us advances at our own pace and believe things in our own time. When you hear the right answers to your questions, it will feel right.

So as you read "Whispering Wings" keep an open mind and if the things I write seem true to you then you should feel it ring as the truth to the very core of your spirit. If you are unsure or you cannot accept this at this time at least you will have heard it from me. You will only comprehend the right information when you are ready.

But as I have said I want everyone to research and find the real truth. If you ever find yourself on a level and don't know where you are, I hope you will remember what I tell you now. In another book I wrote called "Visions or Dreams" I needed to write what I had learned up to that point in my life. I still had so many unanswered questions. Then slowly GOD lifted this veil from my eyes. GOD can lift this veil for anyone at any time, all you have to do is ask and search your soul with all the commitment you can muster. On the other side is our real first home.

HEAVEN is where there is Immediate and Eternal Knowledge. When and if this happens you will understand why you are born, why you picked your mother and father, why you picked your sisters and brothers and why you picked you friends to grow up around. Each one was chosen by you and GOD to help you achieve what your soul needed at the time you and GOD planned your physical life. You will choose a dear and close friend to serve as your Spirit Guide (guardian Angel). Some say this guide is another part of you. Your soul/spirit is always the same but it is more complex. Your body will take on a different form each time you come to this earth. It will always be a human form.

This may be too much for you to believe, just remember this is what GOD showed me. According to some scholars one day this veil will lift for everyone and then everything will "Forever Be Revealed." You will be shown only what you need to know the most. There is no way you can comprehend the whole picture at one time. I was shown the whole picture once and when I tried to remember everything because I knew the importance of what was happening I found I could only remember a few things. I remembered at the time how amazing and how everything made sense now, and just how beautiful the place was.

The sky was the most beautiful brilliant blue and gold. And the grass was also a shade of green I had never seen before. One place had a beautiful black stallion grazing in the green grass. The trees swayed gently in a make believe wind I could not feel, because there was no wind. Everything seemed to be alive, even the flowers in the fields. The flowers swayed to beautiful sounds of music. I remember I could hear the music. There was a large basket (reminded me of an Easter Basket, except really large) setting on the grass. I asked what that is for. GOD said, "This basket represents where you store all of the trials and tribulations and experiences you have until you can sort them out and handle them on your own." That was before God showed me we store all of our experiences and prior lives in our own orb. I guess you could say we store everything in our own basket.

REVELATIONS

W E PICK WHO WE WILL SPEND OUR life with, even if it's just for a little while. It's all a learning stage we must go through. If we could accept this, look how much easier we could accomplish our goals. We pick our children who in turn have written their own charts and have included us in them. We do the same with our parents and friends. We all interact with each other as we each fulfill our own destiny. This is a complicated course we choose and we will always have GOD to show us the way.

He will. All you have to do is ask.

Your chart can be changed along the way if you have accomplished a specific lesson.

Our Guides are always there to help guide us. They try to inspire us. They talk to us and when we think we have an idea or an answer to a problem it is probably our Guide directing us. Have you ever wondered why you changed your mind to drive a certain road and find out later there was a terrible accident on that road, where you would have been. Your Guide can warn you but you may not pay attention. In some cases you may have two guides. If you talk to them ask them their name.

You may be surprised especially if a name suddenly comes to you. Even if it's not their real name just calling to them will make it feel real. God assigns our guides to us. Our guide has no other job but to guide and protect us. Some guides say earth is a crazy tough place for us to come to and learn. This is why we need constant protection, while in the learning state. Spirits/souls lay out their faults and weaknesses in a blueprint and study it frontwards and backwards before a true chart can be formed. Your guide and you along with GOD will select the lessons and steps for you to go through on your journey to earth.

Your guide will be happy to know you are accepting their existence. They won't care if you call them by their right name as long as you call them to help you. They rejoice when you let them know you know they are there.

I asked my guide for a name and Eleanor came to me just as I woke up the next morning.

Then Fred came into the picture. I use to name my cats Fred. When one of them would die and if I got another one I would name him Fred too. Think of a name you always seem to call your pet when you were growing up. That's what I did. So these are the names of who are my spirit guides whether they like it or not. I will find out one day.

My son David drowned when he was 30 years old. I never believed it was him because they wouldn't let me see his body. I was so mad at GOD for letting him die. I thought I had everything covered. I have three sons and I would pray for them every night. Up to this point they had always been safe. Well, that night I forgot to pray, so I immediately thought it was my fault. I wanted to die. I screamed at GOD so hard I know people had to hear me miles away, but I didn't care. I told GOD to take me and bring him back. I meant it.

David comes to me in Visions to comfort me. After he died he came and got me and he took me to where he was to show me he was ok. People I would tell this to thought I was nuts. But I didn't care I could see him and even touch him. Yes, I could even feel his touch.

I needed that more than I could ever explain. I had to know he was really ok. I always tried to hide my feelings from others.

David has finally gone into the light. I now know he had to die because it was charted in his own life's chart.

Just before GOD started lifting my veil and after my son had died, my other son Rick almost died. He was in ICU for 2 weeks and did not have a very good prognosis. I was told he had 10% chance to live. The doctor said he had blood running into his stomach almost as fast as they could pump it out. He also said if blood fills your stomach over ½ ways you usually don't make it. I was walking down the beach talking to GOD and suddenly I started screaming at Him…"Why?" I told him, "You took my baby and You had better not think about taking another son of mine". I don't know why I said such a thing. My heart had been broken so bad when my youngest son had died.

(What a thing to say to my GOD!)

I guess I felt I couldn't survive if something happened to another one of my sons.

The next morning Rick's condition turned completely around and the Doctors were amazed. I thanked GOD. I asked him to forgive me for my arrogance.

I had not been shown any information at this time about charting my life.

I was told by GOD later I had written these things in my chart. David and Rick had also written the same thing.

GOD lifted the veil again. GOD told me "You have learned a great lesson. You and your sons will not need any further lessons in this pain!"

My guides altered my chart and my son's charts with the help of their spirit guides and our GOD.

The next year my oldest son Bill was taken to the emergency room and he also was put in ICU for 12 days. The doctors expressed concerned for his recovery. His blood count was real low and kept dropping. He had also written this in his chart. This time it was different. This time I told my son he would be OK because GOD had told me. I knew in my heart Bill was not going anywhere just yet. All of our life's courses were changed.

His condition changed immediately and both boys are still doing great to this day. All three of my boys had charted to die early in life, maybe to help me find my way. Sometimes things happen to wake you up. We must accept it that everyone writes their own chart. This chart is a course of learning for each of us. So you really can't judge others for the way they live or act sometimes.

GOD knows accepting this will really be hard for us to do. But if we finally accept we each chart our own course we will finally be able to accept this. Consider the homeless person and what that person must go through. Who are we to condemn them? They evidently wrote being homeless into their own charts and they must learn from their experiences and correct them. Not you.

That does not mean you can't help them. Remember one thing, your personal Guide can petition on your behalf to have your chart altered if it's for your own good.

This can be done if you accomplished a goal and there is no further reason to keep trying. You chose to come to Earth and you can do it more than once. This is not a requirement from GOD. It's your choice. If you are here it's because you chose to come here. You can't blame anyone else.

Some like the other side so much they will never come back here.

I have had to experience three more tragic deaths since my sons' incidents. My husband and I lost our dear friend of many years. We both rejected his admission he was dying. We could not accept it. Stuart would tell Fay they don't believe I am dying. We didn't. Stuart and Fay were our closest friends. He told us he had an incurable tumor which could not be operated on. I knew God could cure him. I looked up every cure I could find and give it to him. I didn't know then he had written it into his chart. I prayed and prayed for God to help him. Stuart died within four months and we were devastated again. Last year Fay called me on Christmas morning. This was her first Christmas without Stuart. She said she had a red rose in bloom on her rose bush. Their last name is Rose. None of us had heard from Stuart since he died. I went outside and looked around and found a red camellia in bloom at this same time. This was 20 degree weather and this camellia bush had never bloomed. Stuart did contact us. Your loved ones can contact you in strange ways from the other side.

Jack was my brother in law and also a close friend of ours. He had a heart attack and left us so quick. His family took it so hard and so did we. He was my sister Joyce's ex-husband. They had been together for about 20 years before they got a separated, so we were friends and we couldn't blame either one for the divorce. Jack was more than a partner in business and a true friend. He was family. He could have been president! Jack was very smart especially with words. We all took his death really bad.

Then the one thing I thought I would not be able to take. The death of my younger brother, also named David. My youngest son David had been name after him. David had a head stroke and stayed in a coma for 1 week before he died. He was hard-headed sometimes and so lovable at other times. We were lead to believe if he went to a nursing home he would have a chance for us to take him home. But it doesn't work that way. I found out when they go to a nursing home that is the end of the line. David could see us but he couldn't talk. One day I brought a rose in a vase and a card into the room for everyone to sign. David would always bring me a rose for my birthday or he would just bring a rose to show he loved me. The vase set next to his bed. As Linda started to sign the card first, the vase suddenly burst. We all looked at David, his energy had burst that vase and he had tears in his eyes. I still have the vase. I feel he didn't want us to give up on him and I knew he was mentally not ready to die. He died the next day. The only reason I am telling you about these deaths is because they are the last people who died before God lifted the veil. Now I know they all planned their lives and their deaths. I was privileged just to have known them and I feel they all played a big part in my life too as they helped me to fulfill my own chart. It was right after my brother's death when GOD started to let me remember the things HE had shown me on the levels long ago. I feel like I am being pushed to write about what HE told me.

HE wants HIS WORDS published now.

My WALK WITH GOD
ON THE 7TH LEVEL

God first words to me while on this level

GOD IS THE SOURCE OF ENERGY THAT **controls the Universe. God is not a person but a source of energy. Out of this source of energy Jesus was formed in the flesh to deal with the state of man. Individuals must find and correct their faults and not develop new ones. This must be accomplished before going to the next step. These steps are hard for man to accept until they have understood and accepted a state of awareness in order to comprehend. Desires and habits of the flesh hold back mind awareness. If awareness develops while in the state of man, you may be able to advance faster to a higher level, depending on each individual. If you do**

not become aware of the mind being more important than the earthly body of the flesh and you let the flesh control your mind and you die you may have to return to the flesh again for another chance to find awareness. Overindulging in any manner is a form of sin to your body as well as to your mind.

I didn't think I could take anymore and I was lying in bed one night and couldn't sleep. My head had been killing me and my temples felt like they were going to explode. I suddenly felt myself rise above my body and I was looking down at myself lying on the bed. My husband was asleep next to me. I was shocked at what was happening.

At the same time I was amazed.

I rubbed my temples real hard again, which every time I did this it made my temples strain beyond hurt. And suddenly my body rose up above my house. I could actually see my roof. So I did it again. This time I could see the earth and the moon. By this time my temples were passed bursting. I went up another level, which was black and another one. I was too curious to quit and I went up one more level. This time it was different. My temples quit hurting and any pain I had been feeling was completely gone. The level was not black. It was a brilliant blue and a more brilliant gold. I could see myself standing next to a figure of someone who never spoke but still he communicated with me.

GOD told me, *"Some levels are black because souls are transiting through death to this side. Some have not accepted death. Others may be in a coma having their souls knocked out of their body by an accident or by some other reason. They will stay in the levels until they return to their* bodies, this will happen when they are ready if it is not their turn to die. Some will need special treatment!"

Then he told me I would never get cancer because he was going to tell me why people get cancer. He said, "When a person lets something eat at them like a grudge or hate for another person they need to just give it up and let it go. Don't let it eat at you. There is evil on earth which is just looking for an excuse to invade your soul and your body. Evil is always around and it will grab onto you and destroy you if you allow it. So now you know. If you don't allow Satan to come near, you will not get cancer and I know you will not".

He also showed me the steps everyone must go through on earth and what happens when we return. He took his hand and drew an object in the sky and explained the three steps up and the three steps down. "The steps represent the challenges you chose for yourself on a chart with God's help and what happens when you achieve your goals. You even choose your own death and when you will return Home." There are some things I remembered from the first experience but most of it I forgot. I could not remember everything when I woke up. Until God lifted the veil and I slowly started remembering everything I was shown.

My first experience on the other side was with the 7 levels. I was shown on the seventh level how everyone ever created is still around which includes our presidents, famous people, as well as each one of us. I thought this was a little far out.

Then one day I was told by my granddaughter Sharon, who was 12 at the time that she had seen David who had come to her in a dream the night before. This was David, my son who had drowned when he was 30 years old. We could never prove he had been murdered. We have an idea who killed him but we could never prove it. David asked her where I was because he needed me to look at the papers given to him to fill out and he told her the Elders wanted me to be with him when he went before the council. David told her he was in a hurry and he had this meeting with these elders who could help him which was really important and he needed to plead his case to them. He said they were trying him today.

The Elders were trying to decide whether to let him return to earth or not. This is not normally done so early after death. So David said he would really have to convince the Judges he must return because he died before his goals were accomplished. These important men were assigned by GOD to judge each one of us. They have the power to change our charts.

David also told her his judges were hard but fair.

He said their names were;

Theodore Roosevelt,

Michael Angelo,

Leonardo Devin chi, and

Christopher Columbus.

I thought that was the craziest thing I had ever heard.

That was until I was told there are Judges on the other side and our guides also approach them on our behalf.

They consist of people like Theodore Roosevelt and many other important famous souls.

As I remembered her dream, I was totally amazed. Actually I was stunned.

I have also learned there are 7 levels on the earth plane. There are so many levels within the levels. There are Levels within the Levels on the Other Side as well as on Earth.

So many people are shown only what they can understand and absorb. That is why GOD only let me remember parts of what I was shown when he felt I was ready to understand and comprehend it.

The First Level is the Earth

This is the physical world. This is the only level where we bear a physical body which houses and protects our soul. This is the level where we go to help perfect our soul.

A soul learns at a faster rate in the physical realm than on any other level. That is why you come here. This is done to complete your oneness with GOD. But there are other levels on the first level.

The Second level is where Hell exists

This is a gray level. Only souls exists here who deny there is a GOD. Or those souls who have never heard there is a GOD. A physic once said she was told when you die be sure and go through the right door. She said only the souls who do not believe in GOD will always take the left door. These souls will go straight back to earth to reincarnate again. Souls who may believe in GOD but have never accepted Him may stay on this level until they are ready to advance to another level. The souls who are of Satan are considered dark souls and will never go to Heaven. Their main purpose is to bring down the white entities because they do not believe there is a GOD. This may be true and I will remember it in case it is true. But the Second Level also includes other levels where souls go until they graduate to a higher level. These are souls who don't know where they are or that this event is even possible. They have either not accepted GOD or they will stay on this level, kind of like an indoctrination area until they are helped by other souls to understand and advance to a higher level. Prayers will help these souls leave this level and advance to a higher plane. We need to help all those we love to get off this level and we can do this with prayers.

The Devil also is on the first level his main job is to stop us from going back to GOD. He will do everything in his power to achieve this. He is also everywhere on earth and in he can be in any form.

My Son David took me to this level when he first died. It is a gray level for sure. I remember, everything was dark and it was hard to see. There were different rooms and he took me on a short tour. We were in a warehouse looking area and there was a young man there loading something onto a dock inside of a building. He looked at me and I recognized him, but he didn't seem to know me. He said, "What is she doing here? She can't be here." David replied, "She's OK! She is with me". On these levels there is no air for breathing, so I could not stay long.

So for that reason I had to leave. I think this is what the person meant as to why "She can't be here". When I woke up I remembered who he was. He was the son of a friend of our family. This boy had died two years before when a motorcycle he was on hit a vehicle head on.

He didn't remember me but I remembered him. I went to his funeral. A few years later his brother also died a tragic death and I also went to his funeral. These were Gene Champs sons.

There was another time when my oldest brother, Jimmy, who had already died and I thought had crossed over came to me in a dream.

I was surprised to see him because he was one person who had never come to me after he died. I always wondered why he had not done that.

Well, I asked him "Jimmy why you still here, you died years ago and you should have gone on?" He said, (As though Carol was not my name), "I know Carol had 12 major challenges to go through, and she has already gone through most of them and handled them and I just wanted to stick around to see how she handles the other three." I never told anyone about what he said; I just know I cannot forget what he said and I wonder what else he was waiting for me go through. When I was young Jimmy would teach us how to draw beautiful spirals and spheres. He was the oldest of eight kids so I think he did it to keep us occupied. He would make me draw them over and over until it was perfect. I think they were called octagons or hexagons.

I noticed in the research on orbs they had pictures and cross sections of orbs and they looked like what my brother use to get us to draw.

I now wonder if he was digging deep into his spirit while he was drawing them.

This is what Jimmy kept making us draw. It was fun and as you can see this drawing could go on forever. Some research says that Orbs are other world beings from other dimensions. It's even said that some Orbs are extraterrestrial beings keeping watch on the "goings on" on planet earth.

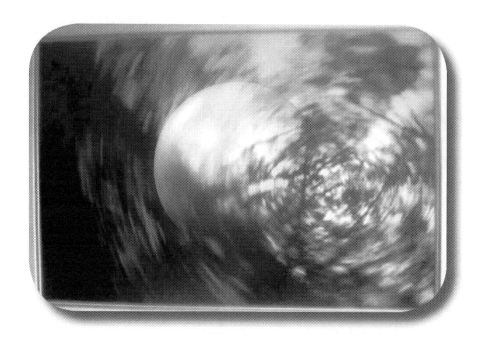

*This copy of a cross section of an actual orb
reminded me of Jimmy's drawing.
Robert, one of my brothers also died but has never
shown himself to me. I fill he may be stuck in one
of these levels. One day I will find out why.*

The Third level is where peace and great beauty exist.

This is a level of beautiful, brilliant colors. The colors are so vivid. They were so striking, so bright and so unforgettable. Every color of the rainbow exists.

There were even colors I could never imagine. If you accept going to this level before you die you soul will go straight here depending on how much you have grown spiritually. You will stay here until the soul desires to grow more towards GOD's eternal oneness, which is everyone's main goal.

When you first come to this level you may think you are in Heaven because of the beauty and your friends and family will be there to greet you. Some stay here because they don't think it could be any better than this. This is where children come to when they die on earth. They will wait here for their friends and family.

If you are pregnant on earth and have a miscarriage your baby will come straight to this level, Jesus will be there with them and they will wait for you to return. Others will care for this little soul completely. If it is written you will get pregnant again and this same little soul will be waiting to be born again, but if you don't get pregnant again, then you will meet your baby when you go back to the other side. This child will grow up on the other side while it waits for you to come home. The child will age with you.

Some advanced souls go to a higher level depending on their desire and awareness. Souls can go from level to level to help others to advance.

David also took me to this level one time. He came and got me and said, "I am going to show you how we dance in Heaven".

I was in a full white gown and he was in a tuxedo. We danced across beautiful blue skies and fluffy white clouds. We floated with graceful moves back and forth to the sounds of the most amazing music I had ever heard.

It seemed like we danced for hours. The cutest little girl with blonde ringlets in her hair followed us, laughing and holding onto my gown and dancing along with us. Just as suddenly as David appeared he was gone.

All animals reside here. They love each other no matter what kind of animal they are. You can go to this level any time you want; some souls seem to stay here forever because they are so close to animals. Of course, your own pet can be with you anytime you choose or they can reside with you on other levels. Your animal(s) will greet you when you return, so remember you will see them again.

I had another incident that happened to me last year that is worth mentioning. I was taken to a level by Mr. Shankle. He died in 1976. I didn't know him that well. He was the father of a close friend of ours. My sister Barbara was married to his son years ago.

Mr. Shankle asked me to please tell his wife he has prepared a room and was waiting for her to come home. He tried to show me the room but I could not stay there very long. I felt I could not breathe. We walk down a hall and the hall started to get real narrow. The longer I stayed there the worse I got. He didn't want me to leave until I told him I would do it. I said I would try.

I did say I would tell his son, Dale and Robert his grandson, but I didn't know if I could tell his wife such a thing. How can you tell someone to give up on life? Well, I couldn't bring myself to tell either of them. The next week he came to me again and he wanted to know what the hold up was. He was serious too. So I told my sister Barbara and she told them for me. She did see them more than I did. Mrs. Shankle died a few months later, so now she is with him on the 3rd Level.

She was in her 90's when she died.

The Fourth Level

This is another level of higher learning and where beauty surpasses the third level. On this level records of everyone born and charts of their lives exist in the Hall of Records. Also every book or works of art ever written or created on Earth is stored here. If you come to the Hall of Records there is one room where you stand and ask a question and the answer immediately comes to you. Some call it virtual reality.

Everyone's chart is also located in the Hall of Records as well as records of every life you ever lived.

Also on this level is where research is done for all medicines, technology and anything imaginable and you will also find this is where doctors and scientists project information in order to help those on earth.

Another amazing thing I learned was our spirit can visit our orb anytime it wants. The spirit does this while you are asleep. This is considered the cycle of life; some say the circle of life or full circa. Your spirit remains in this orb until the spirit becomes one with God.

When the two becomes one it experiences the greatest love of all. It will be similar to when two people come together and obtain the essence of one. Only Gods love will be magnified beyond comprehension. God let me experience this feeling twice. Both times were on the 7th level.

The Fifth and Sixth Levels

The levels are shared by teachers and Angels. Angels never reincarnate. GOD created Angels for one purpose and that is to fight Satan and to help us when we need them. The Angels fight many of our battles for us and we may never even know it. Angel come in different levels too, depending on their job.

Teachers, of the highest advancement, have duties here to help those on lower levels to advance towards GOD. The teachers love to help others to advance to a higher level. Along with the Angels they help others advance towards a total oneness with God.

Both Teachers and Angels have specific jobs. I by no means am saying teachers are equal to Angels. Angels have one specific job. There are different levels of Angels.

Teachers that have advanced so high are assigned jobs to help others advance even if it means returning to earth in order to achieve their goals. As I said Angels do not incarnate but do come to earth when they are called upon to help us achieve our goals.

The 7th Level

When a soul reaches the 7th level the soul has become one with GOD and will experience peace and pure magnified love.

This is where souls are reunited with our GOD in complete perfection. You will be absorbed into the ultimate of Peace and Love. This level also contains colors more beautiful and never seen on any other level. This is Eternity. This is the level GOD took me to in order to explain life and Eternity. This is where I received completely awareness of my purpose. On this level you are in GOD's white light. This is why I felt no pain and I felt pure LOVE. This is where I was when GOD took me by the hand and showed me all the wonders of the universe.

He showed me the purpose of the other planets. He showed me the purpose of other universes. The purpose of loving everything GOD ever created. This level was so peaceful and filled with so much love and beauty I never wanted to leave. The sound of the beautiful music seeped into my soul and is unimaginable to describe. It will never leave me. It was here when I was told to tell others what I have seen. I was told it will help me and it will help them, whether they are on Earth or whether they are in Heaven.

This is the level where I experienced God's love on two different occasions. First was when he explained his plan to me. Then he came to me one night and took me to the seventh level again. This time I was in a room with a lot of people. These people were of all races and genders. There was an excitement in the room and we were told someone very important was coming in to grant us our greatest desire. Elvis entered the room. He walked over to an elderly black man who was bent over and dressed in work clothes. The man was crying. They never spoke out loud, but they were communicating. Elvis touched his shoulder and suddenly the man smiled and changed into a young well to do, well off, finely dressed man. The man smiled at everyone as he left the room. Suddenly Elvis walked to me and without saying a word out loud he asked me what my greatest desire was. I said, "I want to feel God's great love again." He was puzzled at first and then he smiled as he walked right through me. At that moment I was filled with the same pure esoteric feeling I had felt before. This feeling of comfort and ecstasy remains with you for a long time.

This is the pure love of God.

Then I was told I had to return because my mission was not finished on earth. I didn't want to leave, but I knew I have a job to do.

So, this is my purpose in life.

Being on this level was like standing on top of the Universe. On this level I knew everything from the beginning of time until the end of time. Time was endless. I was allowed to experience the ultimate love that lets you feel the oneness with God.

I felt the love of all the advanced souls who had made it back. I knew every soul and felt their love and needs. I felt the hurt coming from the lost souls who were still wandering in the dark levels. I felt the longing to help each one of them. Just as suddenly as I came I left.

The Drawing

This is one of the drawings I drew when I awoke from my dream. These are the steps and levels GOD revealed to me that night when I had my out of the body experience. HE drew this diagram in the sky with a wave of HIS hand. HE also drew an X at the top of the dome to show me where I was at this particular moment in time. It took a long time to know what He meant when he told me this was where I was at that moment. I was on the 7th level where peace and pure love reigns.

7 LEVELS OF CREATION

1st *Level*
Created a Course /Chart

2nd *Level*
Created the Universe

3rd *Level*
Created Plans

4th *Level*
Created Souls and placed them on Planets

5th *Level*
Created other Dimensions

6th *Level*
Created Reincarnation
Created Incarnation on other Planets

7th *Level*
Merged All Creation

The Fifth Ray – *Purple*

This is the Ray of Truth. The more you learn the truth the more you will want to know. The Truth will feel right down to the core of your soul. This ray emits purple energy.

The Sixth Ray – White

This Ray is the Ray of Protection. It protects you from all negativity. It's the White Light. So always surround yourself with the White Light of GOD especially when you need protection.

The Seventh Ray – Gold

The Seventh Ray is a history of all you have accomplished for the Glory of GOD.

It sums up all you have achieved in this and any other life. Your Spirit on this Level or Ray takes on a purple to Gold Ray. On this level all of your experiences over lifetimes will come together for GOD's glory.

There are 7 levels below the Earth Plane
There are 7 levels on the Earth Plane and
There are 7 levels above the Earth Plane.

The Bottom Ray is a continuance of the
Golden Purple Ray

Now this is the bottom level where GOD had to explain everything to me until I could comprehend the answer. This bottom level is when we return home to the other side to access our successes and failures and to re-evaluate our lives.

We will be reunited with our family and friends and even our pets. Our Spirit takes on a Golden to Purple Shade of Ray.

On this level all of your experiences will come together to be evaluated for the Glory of GOD.

Why Do We Dream?

*I*HAD ALWAYS WONDERED ABOUT THE PURPOSE OF *Dreams.*
Then my dream question was answered like this.

Dreams are a way to connect to GOD. It is what God planned for our spirit to have a place to go and get regenerated in love to give it strength for the next day. In our dreams we can remember our lives before we came here. We can re-visit our home on the other side and make sure we are on the right path. But you have to know this in order to take advantage of this great source we have available to us. This way God can keep in touch with each of us.

Through sleep we recharge our batteries for our body as well as our soul. Rest refresh's our body and God refresh's our soul or spirit. Our soul never sleeps. Our soul can do a lot more without the weight of our physical body. This way God protects our Soul as we rest our bodies. The soul and spirit are one in the same. The only thing different from our spirit is our mind.

Our mind rules the flesh and will only recognize the spirit when you teach it to accept it. One way to do this is to write down everything you can remember as soon as you can. Keep a pad and pen next to you bed. You will forget what you dreamed within a few minutes after you are fully awake. Once you mind accepts the spirit is real it will accept it and the two will become one. When this happens you will be able to learn and remember what happens while you are asleep.

You know how sometimes you feel like you are falling and your body jumps and wakes you. This is your soul re-entering your body, because you were about to wake up. Your soul will always be with you when you are awake.

The Hall of Records is on the other side. Your chart you created before you came to Earth is kept there. When you sleep your soul may go to the Hall of Records and review your chart. Your soul/spirit may want to see if you are on track or whether you need to change directions.

You will also see friends and your spirit guides.

Your soul/spirit is always aware of your goal. The mind may never remember, unless something triggers the memory. Your mind deals with the present life. Our problems or frustrations of the day may be released and de-solved in dreams. As for nightmares, these are released in dreams of prior life situations that were never resolved and can be released as your nightmares.

You can ask GOD to release any bad or recurring nightmares or dreams into the White Light. He will take them away. It is also possible, if you in this life suddenly develop a disease or if you have terrible pain unexplainable by doctors that you may have had this disease or terrible pain in another life.

It could have been the reason you died in another life. It is also possible you are at the same age that you were in your other life. Ask God to release your pain into the white or green rays of light. So remember, you can be healed. If you need to be healed ask GOD to release your pain or problems into the healing Green Light. If you want knowledge ask GOD to bring you into the Purple Light of Knowledge. If you need protection from evil ask God to surround you with his Blue Light of protection. Of course the White Light will also protect you too, because it is the Pure Love of God.

The White Light of GOD will give you pure love and incorporates all the lights.

HALL OF RECORDS

EVERYTHING EVER WRITTEN AND PRINTED ON EARTH is stored in the Hall of Records or the other side. These records can be accessed from either side.

This leads me to believe my four sisters and I were teachers on the Other Side and we must have needed certain things published in order to affectively teach everyone.

So I feel this must be one of our challenges, and we must accomplish these goals on earth because we needed them in Heaven.

The only way to accomplish this was to come to the earth in order handle this task. So I tell those who love to write or feel a need to write to just do it. Write as though you were teaching someone on earth and/or on the other side. You have got to admit it's a very interesting idea. There's no room for doubt or self-pity. Everyone gets sidetracked just as I do. It's in our nature, plus we all have other obligations we must tend to first.

Ask GOD to help you put him first.

Also ask GOD for his help and let him guide you. When you return (in the blink of an eye) you will be happy you accomplished something which may have been one of your goals in the first place.

Your time and days are numbered on this earth and that too is written on your chart. They are numbered because you have already written when and how you will leave this earth.

Life plays tricks on you! You get depressed!

It's like a curtain covers your spiritual eye. Have you ever heard of the "third eye"?

By looking through the third eye you can enter your soul, thus finding your spirit. It is like going through a portal to the Other Side. Answers are revealed to you as you need to know, only when you are ready and of course you have to want and you need to ask, it took me 30 years or more to get this far. Every day I learn something new.

GOD will reveal his secret to you too.

All souls retain the age of 30 years old on the other side. I don't know why. I guess you probably look your best and it is usually the best time of your life.

Everyone is born for a specific reason.

Everyone is born with Free Will.

This is where our Free Will comes into the picture. Our free will helps us to choose whether to react to a situation with anger, violence or love.

Accepting a situation and knowing beforehand you had picked this situation before you came here should let you learn and feel and accept the consequences of the tragedy or problem even happiness. This situation happened because

you and GOD felt you needed this experience. GOD does not put hardships on us.

These hardships were chosen by each of us before we came here. We must correct and learn from the lessons while on Earth.

As I said we also pick and we chart our own death and when we will go home. So when you die and go Home it is written and only GOD can change it. Knowing this aspect of it is the only way I could even start to accept my sons' death. How can I feel anything different accept happiness for him? Plus I know I will see him again on the other side.

At the beginning of this book I told you about Orb's.

I know now GOD was trying to wake up my Spirit by showing me ORBS. I believe He was trying to get me back on the right path in my chart. The knowledge He gave me has been lying dormant too long.

The possibility of a spirit in a floating spiral observing and showing itself under different circumstances to other living souls is amazing in itself. It shook me up that is for sure.

I believe we all exist in an orb. Each of our lifetimes is contained in a single complex multi-tasking orb. Within this orb is my own little universe. Within my orb is every lifetime I have ever known. It also includes my growth with GOD on my journey to the 7th Level!

Each one of us possesses his or her specific orb. Everyone has an individual soul within their physical body. It is quiet as its mind rules its body. Because of this some find it hard to except anything out of context of their own logical mind. Your spirit lies quietly awaiting its discovery. Until each one

of us experience part of the Universal Mind of God which is the mind that controls and rules everything, he/she will not be able to see past his/her own logical mind and ideas which were learned or taught to that soul in his/her lifetime.

Orbs play and important role in understanding Gods plan for us. The more the spirit learns and grows the larger the orb becomes. What a realization of ones-self to accept. A logical mind will find the ideas in this book very hard to accept. The problem is each of us thinks we are our own mind and we think we are in control of ourselves and our lives.

When we give in and realize we are only a small part of the Great Universal Mind, which is GOD, and we turn our souls over to GOD, then and only then can we find peace and contentment.

There was another experience I had one night. All week was very hectic at work. To top it off everyone was getting sick with the flu. I kept saying over and over "I can't get sick I don't have time to get sick".

Well, Thursday came along and sure enough I started feeling really sick. I went home and still had payroll to do and soon as that was finished I went straight to bed. I expected to feel so bad the next day I would stay home. During the night, someone came and got me. He didn't speak but I knew what he said. He said, "Come with me". We ended up in a large room.

I never saw anyone else. In the center of the room was a round table which was white. I was told to lay face down onto the table. He told me to turn my face to the left which I did. Suddenly the table became a bright light it went right

through my body. Then I was told to turn my face to the right. The right side of my face is where I really hurt. Then again the bright light came on and went through my body a second time. The pain was gone.

I was then told I could leave. No more words were spoken. The next day I woke up and noticed I felt good. I was no longer sick in any way. I remember what had happened and went to work and told everyone. I felt I had been healed by someone who loved me. It is just one more thing I will never forget. There are no words to describe the feeling of wellness and energy I felt. Thinking about that table is unbelievable.

It seems beyond comprehension what is available to us. This experience happened to me before the use of lasers was commonly known to us as they are today. But my illness was the flu or either a bad cold. All I know is I had a fever and I was aching all over when I went to bed. I felt completely well when I woke up the next morning.

What a miracle it will be when they figure out how to cure these kinds of illnesses by just laying down onto a table and let the healing light cure us.

In the Spiritual Realm

OUR SIGNATURE IN THE SPIRIT REALM IS a form of energy.

Each of us radiates a specific color and sound.

Just as each one of us has a different set of fingerprints here on earth. Each one of us radiates a different sound and color. I am different from any other person.

Fascinating!

That is what makes each of us different.

God loves every soul equally. When a soul realizes this, that soul emits a light which attracts other souls. On earth feelings travel in frequencies, like radio waves travel. Depression and hate is in the lowest level. You can bring yourself to a higher level and get out of the lower level and if you will accept this you can do it on your own and get away from depression. Everyone experiences depression at one time or another.

Sometimes when I get depressed or highly emotional, I try to bring myself out of it by saying any phrase like 5148 or "get me out of this level please!" I just say it over and over and suddenly I will be out of that depressing level. I know this may sound silly because that is what I thought the first time I heard it. But you know it works. So try it sometimes and it will work for you too, just have faith. Of course you don't have to say 5148, just pick something you are familiar with and say it over and over and over. It breaks the level.

Ask God to take your hand and pull you up out of this level and he will, that is the surest way.

Levels exist on the waves similar to sound ways and microwaves. It's interesting how frequencies exist. There is so much to learn.

Planets and Spiritual Development

Between lives in the flesh the spirit will visit one or more planets trying to weed out all the little sins it has developed or learn knew lessons. This will help per-fect their oneness with GOD.

I was told the true purpose of the other planets. No matter how hard man develops and manages to get to the other planets they will never find what the true purpose for the planets creation is until the receive complete awareness. NASA has mapped the Solar System. They also report Saturn is 844 times bigger than the Earth. Even the winds on Neptune have been recorded at 1400 MPH. The true purpose of the other planets is to allow a spirit to go to for various teachings and lessons they must per-fect in order to grow towards pure love.

Earth - *The Spirit experiences existence in The flesh. This gives each of us the opportunity to learn fast.*

Mars - *The Spirit learns to distinguish and cure any hostile feelings it may have.*

Venus - *Helps to teach the Spirit perfect Love.*

Uranus - *Helps the Spirit not to give great importance to problems.*

Jupiter - *Leads the Spirit towards restraint.*

Mercury - *Lets the Spirit review each life.*

Saturn - *Spirit worships GOD with pure Love.*

Neptune - *Spirit finds tranquility.*

Pluto - *Helps Spirit find re-direction.*

LUCIFER

WHILE I WAS IN LIMBO ON ONE of the dark levels I became nervous and started to doubt why I was there. I thought things like "What am I doing here and what if I get stuck here!" I left this level quick, never wanting to return.

While in this state the following was revealed to me. *From the beginning of time and until the end of time there is one Angel who will have dominance over the physical earth. You should always be aware of his presence. His main plan is to prove he is more powerful than God and he will do everything in his power to convince all people of this. We all need to be aware of his plans. His main goal is to control the earth and recruit all the souls and stop them from becoming aware of the other side. He wants you to stay on his level to be controlled by him.*

He plans to rule by being completely in control of all spirituality, next he will try to control the earth by controlling our economics. And last of all he will try to control all the people who are in charge of controlling others.

He will be disguised in many forms and his identity and his plans will be hidden from our eyes.

A lot of us will be fooled by his plans and will fall into his trap, even though we are all warned and told about it in the Bible.

His plan is hidden from view in an invisible society. He controls this society from within an inner circle and all his brotherhood work together to enforce his goal as masters of the secret doctrine. People who follow this doctrine are unaware of his ultimate goal. Beware!

A veil will protect him until his time is up. This Angel is found in the Bible. Don't be fooled because he goes by many names.

His name is **Lucifer.**

"For nothing is secret, that shall not be made manifest, neither anything hid that shall not be made known" Luke 8:17

"Ye shall know the truth and the truth shall set you free" John 8:32

"The wise shall understand" Daniel 12:10

Rules to Obtain
ULTIMATE Success

IN ORDER TO ACCQUIRE SOUL COMPLETENESS:
You must love GOD with all your heart.
Never willfully hurt another soul.
You must accept others for what they are.

Then you go after what you want with an attitude of respect for others and you must always be honest in all your dealings.

Always be thankful for what you have.

Keep a Happy Heart and it will rub off on others.

We are all unique vessels in which the power of GOD flows through us to others as well as to ourselves. When we take the opportunity to come into this world we relish the idea of being able to be able to enjoy and develop our senses.

Our eyes let us see the beauty God has created for us to enjoy while we are here. The sunrises and the sunsets are so beautiful and make us feel closer to home.

To be able to see and absorb the energy of a child's smile is so rewarding and comforting. You must experience it to appreciate it. A child can change a bad day into a good day.

Only with your eyes can you look deep into another's soul and feel their love or hurt, and you can only do that and have those feelings on earth.

The sense of smell can only be enjoyed here. Can you imagine not being able to smell roses or other flowers and think about the smell of something good cooking or even the smell of a good perfume or good cologne?

They say only on earth can you actually enjoy the touch of another being. Can you imagine loving a puppy or kitten? Only an animal can return love with no strings attached. The hug of a loved one or child can soothe or break your heart.

Then last is the power of hearing. GOD made sure we could hear so we could be reminded of home. When you hear certain music it can remind you of the beautiful music in God's kingdom.

Only through our senses can we totally enjoy life.

The rules God instills in us will totally guide us along the way. If you keep these rules GOD will infuse you with the knowledge you need to succeed in life.

So the more you learn the more you know and if it feels right in your soul, then go with it.

Others who want to know will follow you if they are ready to learn. If they are not ready they may not follow your lead, but they will have definitely felt your spirit and they will retain it until they are ready to find their own stairway to GOD. I know what I felt when my son David came to me in a vision and hugged me so hard to comfort me when after he died. I don't know exactly where we were but I know the feeling was real.

LESSONS LEARNED

Aﾍ FTER MY FIRST EXPERIENCE WITH GOD ON the levels over 40 years ago where he guided me through the steps of my very existence, I find myself continually looking for any similar experience just to make sure I have not missed something of importance. This experience was my near death experience as describe by others who claim they had when they traveled through a tunnel with a bright light calling to them from the end of that tunnel. This is their "Heaven and Back" experience.

This story is my "Heaven and Back" experience.

I have always been able to see a light in a completely dark room and I always thought everyone could see it. This light will get brighter as I focus with all my effort.

Sometimes I can pull this light through me and/or others when praying for their healing. And God heals them.

When my niece died a tragic death before my son died, my world started to shatter which in turn started my quest for God. Karen was Joyce and Jack's daughter. I helped raise her from the time she was born. She was the first child born to any of us sisters so she got all of the attention while growing up. It seems it didn't take long before that happened and she grew up.

She got married and had already had one son and was pregnant with another child when her car went off a cliff in a state park and both she and the unborn baby died.

This was supposed to have been a weekend outing with her family in the park that turned tragic.

This happened after my parents had both died when I was 22 years old. I thought Karen's death was the last straw. I didn't think I could go on. I was unable to attend her funeral because it was in another state, which made it worse. My heart hurt so bad I didn't think I could ever stand it. I guess the worst part was how her parents were taking it.

I pulled the white light through both of them so many times I can't count them. It had to have helped them because Joyce told me Karen came to her and she was adorned with beautiful wings and she assured her mom she was ok.

GOD created the Earth so each of us could experience the different senses only available on Earth. GOD our father, would never send us off into the unknown without a plan and without supervision. He is our father. He lets us choose our problems, our loves, our hurts, even our death. He will never leave us alone.

He has many ways of watching and taking care of his children without our knowledge. The plan is to come home to Him only when these steps have been completed. If for some reason you leave before all are completed, you may have another chance to try again in the future. It will be yours and GOD's decision.

Think how much easier life will be once you can believe this scenario. After my parents died I stumbled through life for years searching for a purpose in life. Then when my son died I wasted another 14 years trying to accept his death. I did not begin to accept his death until God started lifting the veil from my eyes. All I wanted was to bring his killer to justice. But I am not a judge, God is.

Each struggle we have, whether it is because of money, love, marriage, divorce, sickness, and even death, or any other tragedy life hits you with, you will find it will not be more than you can stand. If you recognize that these things are stepping stones God will help you to get past them and get on to the next challenge. You will be surprised how much easier life becomes for you and for others. What we project affects everyone around us. When we realize each one of us is important and is perfect in GOD's eyes we will shed all fears of acceptance by others. No one soul is better than another. Once you accept this unconditionally your inner light starts to shine through. This light is seen by others and gives them inspiration for hope and love. This light and these feelings are projected out and travel in frequencies just like sound waves.

The highest frequency is where love is found.

And as I said before, the lowest frequency is where fear and hate lives. This is the frequency that causes all the problems of the world.

Souls create havoc from this area. The murderers, rapist, thieves, and even just hateful people get stuck on this depressing level. Once you learn the different levels of frequencies, you will be able to control your own feelings and moods by getting to a higher level.

MY SEMATA

THEN THERE WAS THE NIGHT I WAS lying awake around 3:13am. I could not sleep. I kept thing I must get organized, because I have so much to accomplish and I don't know how I was going to do it!

I shut my eyes and suddenly I heard someone say, "It's just a Semata!" I opened my eyes to make sure no one was there. There wasn't. Slowly I shut my eyes again and I said, "I don't even know what a semata is!"

"Chi bang', it means chi bang, do you know what that is?" This had never happened to me before or since.

The words were so clear. It was as though someone was in the room with me. So I said, "I know chi bang is slang for everything!" Well, that did it. "OK, I said I am getting up to find out what you are talking about!" I got up and went straight to the computer. I typed in semata. I wasn't sure how to spell it. It came up to be a Spanish word meaning "week". Then I typed in chi bang, and guess what? Chi bang means the whole part or everything.

So I take it my spirit guides are telling me I can organize my life in 1 week and figure out my goals and finish this book. All I can say is good luck to me. And I am working on it.

It is so important to write down your dreams because they can include so much important information which may help you.

Then there was one

I mirror my own soul

I reflect the Universe

And

I reflect GOD.

I am telling you about this because if you stop and be quiet sometimes and listen you may hear and learn something new from the other side.

A Seed of Thought
From the Author

WHEN YOU READ THESE WORDS AND YOU still doubt your own abilities, remember this:

I was told only the advanced well developed spirit will even attempt to come to earth and to take on a vulnerable body which will house its soul. Only the spirit who has already achieved greatness in the eyes of GOD and who wants to per-fect its spirit will attempt this. This means you are not limited to what you can do or what you can become. You have all this knowledge deep within your own spirit just waiting for you to discover it. Say you wanted to feel more compassionate, you may want to experience being homeless. If you need to feel humility, you may come to Earth and be an ungrateful bigot. Each of us may only need someone to show them a little kindness.

I was also taught God punished woman when he made her bear children. Who are we to say God's motive was for punishment? There's nothing like a small child cuddling up in your arms and especially when that child gives you their innocent sweet smile. A child's smile can change the world.

Everything has a reason to exist and everything happens for a reason. If you feel depressed get off that level and quit feeling sorry for yourself. Reach up to God and take his hand and walk up those steps because you are never alone. It is up to you.

Your main goal is to have experienced every possible feeling and master each one before you can experience a true and complete LOVE never experienced on Earth or anywhere except in Eternity with GOD.

> As the body rests
> The Mind Sighs
> Then the veil lifts
> And the Spirit fly's.

FOUNTAIN OF YOUTH

SOME SPIRITUAL LEADERS HAVE STATED THEY BELIEVE GOD created man twice. When I think about this I guess HE did. HE created man in the spirit and HE created man in the flesh. Man has a life in the flesh which houses the spirit and the spirit continues its life in the spirit on the other side when the flesh is shed.

Adventurers, including Christopher Columbus, sailed the oceans searching for the Garden of Eden. Columbus claims to have found an island near Venezuela which had beautiful mountains rising high into the clouds and the island was filled with exotic flowers and fruit. The island had a perfect all year round temperature. It was rumored on the island there was the fountain of youth but was never found. In today's satellite age, scientist say the Garden of Eden is located in the Persian Gulf. The exact location is found at the mouth of the Tigris and the Euphrates rivers.

The Fountain of Youth is located at the foot of one of the mountains. If you drink from its bubbling spring you will retain the age of 30 years old the rest of your life.

This is why so many people have searched for the Fountain of Youth for thousands of years.

Now where have I heard this before? When on the levels I was told when you get on the other side you will retain the age of 30 for eternity.

One more thing the religious leaders talk about. With the age of computers they can now find and decipher the code of the Bible. Isaac Newton tried to find and break the code before computers were ever invented. Even E. Rips and his company tried and did break the code. They said predictions of the future are hidden in these codes.

Many historical events have been uncovered finding these codes. From the inventions and their inventors to the wars and even the American Revolution in 1776 has been found. I bring this up to show these discoveries were found by men with the use of computers. When you search for the truth through God and if you are lucky enough to receive Gods awareness He will reveal all his codes to you personally.

When I was in the State of Awareness I remember I automatically knew every language from Greek to the original language of Aramaic. I was shown every event from before the event to the time of the event and the future and outcome of the event. I immediately comprehended everything in the Hall of Records. Everything was instantaneous to me. It was like there was no time table involved. I could also see and understand every level and sequence of my own life. The whole experience left me with a feeling I hope will remain with me forever. I do remember I did not want to leave and I look forward to returning.

What I remember the most is this feeling of contentment and the feeling everything is meant to be and everything is right on schedule with God's plan for us. He has everything under control as long as we let him handle it.

Have I Earned Tomorrow

What have I done today?
Have I given any sorrow?
Can I lift my head high enough?
To feel I have earned tomorrow?

Have I made anyone happy?
Who I may have seen today?
Or are they just another face
Who passed along my Way?

Please let me earn tomorrow
By what I do today
Let me take the knowledge you lend to me
And give it out through the Day.

And help me take my Smile, Lord
Which from you I only Borrowed
Until I pass it to another,
Can I Earn One more tomorrow!

Angelica Carol Wright

THE END